Baby Blanket Crochet Patterns Ideas

(*And How to Make Them*)

Table of Content

Introduction

If you're in the market for some baby crochet blanket ideas, we've got you covered. What is cuter than a baby wrapped in a **crochet blanket**? Not much. You'll agree when you see these top crochet baby blankets. These ideas will hopefully help you decide what style, pattern, and feel you want your baby blanket to have.

You will find patterns in different colors and styles, suitable for both boys and girls. They can be created as gifts and are also perfect to donate to hospitals and charities. Most of these crochet blanket patterns also work as lapghans, so you can gift them to nursing homes, not just to babies.

Crochet Cluster Stitch Gingham Blanket

I might not stop crocheting gingham blankets any time soon! If I find two shades of yarn that I think might accomplish the look, I can't help but buy them. That is what happened here with this blanket. These two shades of orange and peach were too perfect together, so I quickly swooped them up and threw them into my cart.

Now, if I only was as speedy as actually making the blanket. I've had this yarn sitting on my shelf for about 6 months or more and finally decided to get after it and turn it into a blanket. I wasn't sure which stitch to use for this one, so I did a practice swatch, which is essential for any of my gingham blanket patterns.

MATERIALS

- Finished size of blanket 36 X 36 inches.
- 1 Skein Hobby Lobby "I Love This Yarn" in Mango
- 1 Skein Hobby Lobby "I LOVE This Yarn" in White
- 2 Skeins Hobby Lobby "1 Love This Yarn" in light peach
- Size K Hook
- Scissors
- Tapestry Needle

SPECIAL STITCH: CLUSTER DC2TOG. YO (yarn over), Insert hook into designated space, YO, pull up a loop, YO, pull through 2 loops, YO, insert hook into the same space, YO, pull up a loop, YO, pull through 2 loops, YO, pull through all 3 loops left on hook.

PATTERN

Chain 96 in Light Peach

ROW 1: SC in second CH from hook and in next 4 spaces for a total of 5 SC. Pull through in 5th SC with White. SC next 5 spaces with white, carrying the light peach along and crocheting over the strand. In the fifth SC, pull through with light peach. SC next 5 spaces with light peach carrying the white along and crocheting over the strand. Continue alternating every 5 spaces to the end of the row. Chain 2 and turn.

ROW 2: 1 DC into the top of the first SC of the row below with light peach, this counts as your first cluster stitch. Cluster in the next 4 SC making sure you have brought the white around the end of the work and you are working over the strand. Just before finishing the cluster, pull through with new color. Cluster stitch the next 5 spaces. Switch back to light peach in the 5th cluster. Repeat alternating the colors to the end of the row. Ch 1 and turn.

ROW 3: Repeat ROW 1. (All SC, alternating colors every 5 spaces)

ROW 4: Repeat ROW 2. (All Clusters, alternating colors every 5 spaces.) In the last stitch, pull through with Mango, cut off the white, continue carrying the light peach.

ROW 5: Repeat ROW 1, with the exception that you are now alternating Mango and Light peach. Use all SC.

ROW 6: Repeat row 4 with same exception as row 5.

ROW 7 and 8: Repeat rows 5 and 6, pulling through with white and cutting off the Mango.

Rows 9-68 Repeat rows 1-8.

Weave in all the ends before you start the border.

In any corner pull up a loop and SC in that space. Then SC into each space around the edge working 2 SC per the sides of DC's and on SC into the tops of the clusters. Work 3 SC into each corner space. When you get back the starting SC, join with a SL ST (slip stitch) chain 2 and turn.

Work a cluster stitch into each SC around the whole blanket, working 2 Clusters into the middle stitch of the corners. Join with a slip stitch at the end of the round, CH 1 and turn.

Work one more row of all SC into each cluster, working 3 SC in between the 2 clusters in the corners. Join with a slip stitch when you return to the beginning stitch. Tie off and weave in all the ends.

Now, before you gift this gorgeous blanket, you may hand wash it if you've found you've had to drag it from place to place with you to get it finished. But, toss it in the dryer and this yarn will soften up an incredible amount and you will love the finished result.

Usually, I let my blankets air dry, laying flat on a towel, but for this one, I had lightly sprayed it with a spray bottle to flatten out the stitches. I tossed it in the dryer when it was still damp, and I was amazed at how the blanket turned out.

I actually posted about it on my Instagram account and asked my followers if they have ever used a dryer and a lot of them had and loved the results. Now, this might be just for acrylic blankets and for Hobby Lobby I love this yarn brand. I haven't tried on anything else. But, if you are wanting an amazing finish, give it a try.

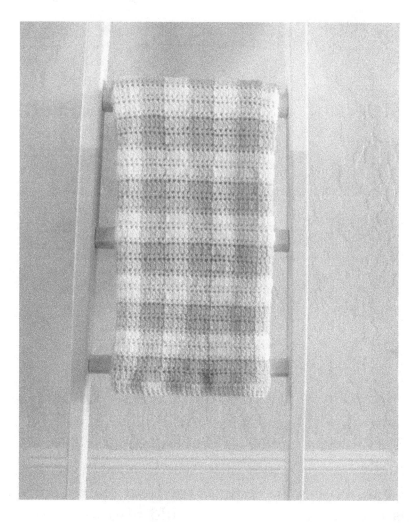

Crochet Sedge Stitch Baby Blanket

I tried out a few different stitches when I was practicing with this yarn and finally settled on the sedge stitch, which seems complicated at first, but is actually pretty straightforward once you get it started. I think the sedge turned out really cool with this cotton, but I think it would also look great in acrylic if you decide to use a different type of yarn!

MATERIALS

Finished size appx. 32 in x 38 in

3 skeins of Bamboo Pop in White

4 skeins of **Bamboo Pop in Lily Pad**

Size G Hook

Scissors

Tapestry Needle

PATTERN

Start with a chain in a multiple of three. (For this blanket I chained 120).

ROW 1: In the second chain from the hook, do a **HDC (half double crochet)** and a **DC (double crochet)**, skip two chains and in the next work a SC, HDC, DC. *Skip two chains and repeat "SC, HDC, DC" into the next space. Repeat * across to the end and there is one chain left. Do one SC and turn.

ROW 2: Chain one (this counts as your first SC), HDC and DC into the top of the SC you just made of the row below. Skip over the DC and HDC, "SC, HDC, DC" into the SC. You'll always be looking for the SC to do your "SC, HDC, DC" into. Repeat the pattern across ending the last stitch with one single crochet. (When you get to the end, you'll have two stitches left, just skip one and SC into the last stitch).

Repeat Row 2 for the rest of the blanket! The more rows you do, the easier it gets to figure out where to work each of your "SC, HDC, DC," but I would suggest doing a small practice swatch before you get started just to make sure you understand how to work the stitch.

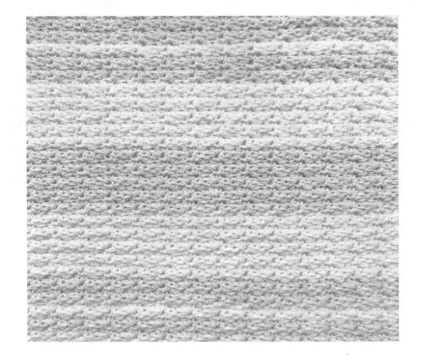

Here is the color pattern I used:
(When you are switching colors, pull through with the new color on your last single crochet at the end of the row when you have two loops on your hook.)

*10 rows White
4 rows Green
2 rows White
4 rows Green
10 rows White
10 rows Green
Repeat from * until you reach your desired length.

BORDER

Before you start the border you'll want to weave in all the ends with a tapestry needle.

For this border you will be making a ribbed stitch look on each side of the blanket, working one side at a time.

Pick either side to work across. Using lily pad, pull up a loop in the corner and chain 3. DC across the entire side. When you are working on the sides it can be hard to figure out how many DC's to work so that the border doesn't ripple or fan out, so you'll want to try to space them out as evenly as you can.

Stop when you reach the first corner, chain 3 and turn. This counts as your first DC.

Insert your hook from front to back around the post of the next DC and work your DC (front post DC). Then, around the next DC, insert your hook from the back to the front and work your next DC (back post DC). Now continue alternating FPDC and BPDC around each DC. When you get to the last DC, work one DC into the top of the stitch. Chain 3 and turn.

Work back across the row with your alternating FPDC and BPDC matching each stitch to start making the ribbed look.

Go back and forth across the row until the border is as high as you would like it (Since this is a lighter yarn, I worked 7 rows for my ribbing – you'll want to pick an odd number so you can work around the whole blanket without having to tie off.)

When you finish the ribbing for the side, do not tie off, simply chain 3, and start working across the end of the blanket, working DCs into the sides of the FPDC and BPDC stitches, and then one DC per stitch. Chain three and turn, then work back across in the same manner you did before and work your ribbed stitch, alternating FPDC and BPDC.

When you finish 7 rows, chain 3, and now work in the same manner up the side, again working one DC per stitch. When you finish working the ribbing up this side and then across the last end, chain 1 and work a SC into each DC all the way around the entire blanket, putting 3 SCs into each corner space. This helps to even everything out and give the corners a nice finished look.

Tie off and weave in the ends.

Crochet Modern Granny Blanket in Peach and Grey

This modern crochet granny blanket is a series of triangles nestled in between each other which gives the blanket a modern feel. This blanket works up fast and is fun to memorize and pick up easily where you left off.

MATERIALS

2 each of *Baby Bee Sweet Delight* in Bashful and Flannel

Size H, 5.00mm hook

Tapestry Needle

Scissors

PATTERN

CH a multiple of 3, then add 1 (3+ 1 is the pattern repeat) to however wide you'd like the blanket. I usually do somewhere between 32 and 36 inches wide for a baby blanket.

ROW 1: 1 DC into 4th CH from hook, *SK next 2 CHs, 3 DC into next CH, repeat * ending with 2 DC into last CH, turn.

ROW 2: CH 3, 1 DC into next DC, (CH 3 counts as first DC), *CH 2, DC3TOG, repeat * ending with CH 2, DC into next DC, DC into top of turning chain, pulling through with new color just before you finish the DC.

NEW COLOR

ROW 3: CH 3, 3 DC in the CH 2 space between the last DC3TOG and 2 DC of the previous row, *3 DC into next CH 2 space, repeat * ending with 1 DC in top of the turning chain.

ROW 4: CH 4, (counts as 1 DC and 1 CH), *DC3TOG in top of each 3 DC of previous row, CH 2, repeat * across and end with CH 1, DC into top of CH 3 turning chain, pulling through with new color.

NEW COLOR

ROW 5: CH 3, 1 DC into DC (the base of the ch 3, the top of the last DC you made), *3 DC in next CH 2 space, repeat * across ending with 2 DC into the top of 3rd chain of the turning chain.

ROW 6: CH 3, 1 DC into the next DC, *CH 2, dc3tog, repeat * ending with CH 2, DC into next DC, DC into 3rd of ch 3 pulling through with new color just before you finish the stitch.

Repeat rows 3-6 until you have a desired length of blanket.

I have made a video for my other Modern Granny Blanket in Peach and Blue that I think can help you understand how to turn this blanket and how to make the DC3tog.

NOTES

Here are a few tips I realized while making this blanket that might be helpful to you.

Since each finished "triangle" (the DC that stack on each other) are nestled in between each other, you will notice that the number of them will be different each color change. For example, I did a small swatch to test the pattern and I ended up with 8 "triangles in one row, then 9 in the next, then back to 8 then back to 9. What I noticed are the rows that have 8 are also the rows where you have 2 DC and the end of the rows. The rows that had 9 "triangles" only had 1 DC on the end.

Below is the border I decided to create and add around my blanket. I did a very zoomed in shot so you could see that I went around the whole blanket working 2 DC in each space. (To start the work with a new color, join in any corner and CH 3, that counts as one of your DC) However, on the sides of the blanket, you will be working 2 DC around the post of a DC. (look closely at the next picture of the finished blanket.)

Now, it might be the yarn I was using, my own personal tension, and yours may be different, but I did have to work a ch in between the 2 DC across the top and bottom. The sides did not need that extra chain. I tried doing it without, because I wanted the stitch to match the sides, but it pulled and puckered. This to me is when you get to be smarter than the pattern. It's much better to work an extra stitch and have it look right, than get your counts exact. Again, you might not have this problem.

For the corners on this round I did add a chain in between the two sets of DC. (2 DC, CH1, 2 DC for the corners)

Continuing on in the same direction for the second round, join with the new color (flannel) and slip stitch one over and CH 3. (This gives the appearance of the first dc into the chain space. Then work one DC into the chain space. CH 2 and work 2 DC into the next space. Repeat this all the way around the blanket, working 2 sets into each corner. When you return back to the original CH 3, slip stitch into the top of that.

Chain 3 and turn your work to go the opposite direction. I hope you are in a corner for this CH 3 is the middle of the shell. DC 4 more times into that space and then SC into the next chain space. You want to work 7 DC into the next chain space, then one SC into the next chain space and repeat this all the way around. However, because I had problems on the sides being closer together than the top and bottom, I only worked 6 DC. I found that working 6 showed no difference, but if I worked 7, the side shells were rippling. Again, this might not happen to you at all. When you return to the corner you started with, work the remaining 3 DC and then slip stitch to the top of the turning chain. Tie off and weave in ends and you are done.

EXTRA TIPS

For the corners, I was able to work a complete 7 DC into each. But, for a crocheter like me who doesn't like to count, (I know, shhh don't tell) I felt so lucky that it just so happened to turn out that way. (sometimes my one SC turns out to be the corner stitch and it looks okay, just not my favorite.) If you are better at math than me and want to make sure you are working the shell into each corner, you may want to add more rounds of 2 DC until you find you are exactly even.

Also, if that last part confused the heck out of you, don't do it! I almost just left the border to be the rounds of 2 DC. I thought it looked good sort of plain. But this is a gift and I decided to make it a little extra frilly.

And, just working all SC around this blanket, switching colors would look great too!

Crochet Sheep Baby Blanket

I'm so happy to see an idea I had in my head actually come to life! I've been thinking about a sheep blanket ever since one of my friend told me his next children's book was going to be called **"Go to Sheep."** How adorable is that?

MATERIALS

Finished size approximately 28 x 28 inches (small lovey size, but you are free to add more border or add more to your base chain to make it bigger.)

3 skeins of **Bernat Baby Softee Chunky in White**

1 skein of Bernat **Baby Softee Chunky in Cozy Grey**

Size L crochet hook

Scissors

Tapestry needle

Graph

PATTERN

Print the graph.

With White, chain 61.

ROW 1: In the second chain from the hook, work one single crochet (SC). Work one SC into each chain to the end. CH 1 and turn.

ROW 2-15: Starting in the first SC, work one SC into each SC across to the end. CH 1 and turn. (60 SC)

ROW 16: Start following the graph at row 1. When introducing grey, pull through with the new color on the last step of the SC, carry the white through and along with you, laying the white along the top of the stitches. Before you finish the last step of the grey, pull back through with the white.

TIP: estimate and unwind a long tail of grey for the one leg and cut off. Use a different strand for the next leg.

TIP: On the 16th row, take note of where the tail for the starting chain is located, that will help you remember what row you are on. Or use markers. Or keep track on the graph.

On the graph, the lighter shaded grey is where you start working the DC2tog clusters, followed by a SC. Simply alternate between the two stitches. Sometimes the row will end with a cluster, sometimes a SC. It doesn't matter. Sometimes you will work into the tops of SC with Cluster stitch, sometimes you will be working SC into SC and Cluster into Cluster. Keeping it freestyle will give you a more wooly look. The clusters won't line up exactly on top of each other and that's okay. Work Clusters and SC in every row that the graph is shaded light grey. This will make sure that you will have clusters popping out on both sides of the blanket.

When you get to the ears, estimate and leave a long tail for each ear. I did not carry the grey yarn along the row.

BORDER

Weave in all ends before starting the border. In any corner, pull up a loop, CH 1 and SC into that same space 2 times. Work one SC per stitch and per row down the sides of the blanket. Work 3 SC's into each corner space. Upon returning to the starting corner, work one SC, slip stitch to the starting SC, CH 1 and turn.

Work 5 rounds of all SC for the border. Tie off and weave in all ends.

To get your blanket looking very straight, lay it out and spritz it with a spray bottle filled with water. You may pin it and then let it dry.

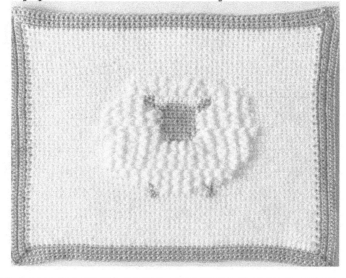

Crochet Modern Dash Baby Blanket

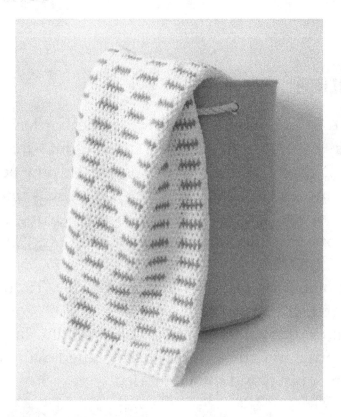

I've been seeing a lot of dashed line patterns on a lot of pillows and rugs lately, and I thought it would be fun to crochet that type of design into a blanket.

MATERIALS

(Stroller size baby blanket, 32 in. x 35 in.)

3 skeins of **Bernat Baby Blanket Tiny** yarn in White

1 skein of **Bernat Baby Blanket Tiny** yarn in Tea Rose

Size H Hook (5.00mm)

Scissors

Tapestry Needle

PATTERN

Chain 103 in White. (To make your blanket larger or smaller, chain any multiple of 8, then add 7.)

ROW 1: Starting in the 3rd chain from the hook, work a HDC in each chain across the row. When you reach the last stitch, pull through with Pink (you should have 3 loops on your hook when you pull through.) Don't cut the White yarn. Chain 2 and turn.

ROW 2: Pull the White yarn behind your work, and crochet over it with 5 HDC's working in between the posts. (To see how to work in between the posts, please watch the video tutorial above. From now on, you will always be inserting your hook in between the posts.) On the 5th HDC, pull through with White.

Carry the Pink yarn behind and work 3 HDCs. On the 3rd HDC, pull through with Pink. Then work 5 HDCs with Pink, carrying the White yarn behind.

Continue the pattern of 5 HDCs of Pink, 3 HDCs of White until you reach the end of the row, always carrying the yarn you aren't using behind your work so you can easily pick it back up again. You should end the row with 5 HDCs of Pink.

When you reach the end of the row, pull through with White on the last stitch, and cut the Pink, leaving a tail that is long enough to weave in later.

ROWS 3 – 5: Work 3 rows of HDC working in between the posts with White, chaining 2 and turning and at the end of each row. On the last stitch of row 5, pull through with Pink.

Repeat rows 2 – 5 for the remainder of the blanket.

I ended up with 25 pink rows when the blanket was the length I wanted. When you reach your desired length, work one row of White after the last Pink row to match the one row of White at the beginning of the blanket.

BORDER

After I tied off and wove in all my ends, I added a front and back post double crochet ribbing border around the edge. Here are instructions for how to add that border, and there is also another video below.

ROW 1: Pull up a loop in any corner and chain 3. DC around the entire blanket, working 3 DCs into each corner stitch.

ROW 2: When you reach the corner you started with, work 3 DCs into the corner, then go around the blanket again, this time alternating front and back post double crochet. A front post DC means you insert your hook from front to back around the post of the next DC and work your DC. A back post DC means you insert your hook from the back to the front and work a DC.

When you get to the corners of this row, you will want to continue the pattern of alternating front and back post double crochet, but you will work three stitches around the corner post.

So, for example, if you get to the corner post and you are supposed to work a front post DC, then work a front post DC, a back post DC, and a front post DC all around that corner post. Then in the next stitch you would continue the alternating pattern, working the opposite of whichever stitch you just used (in this example, you would work a back post DC).

I hope that is not too confusing! Just remember that you are always alternating front and back post double crochet around the whole blanket, you just happen to be working three of those stitches around the same post when you are working the corners.

ROWS 3 – 4: When you finish row 2, work 3 alternating front post/back post DCs into the corner you started with and repeat row 2 two more times around the blanket, until you have four rows total. (Or you can go around as many times as you'd like to get your desired border height. I only had enough yarn to go around 4 times.)

Done!

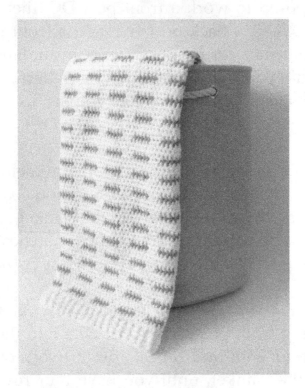

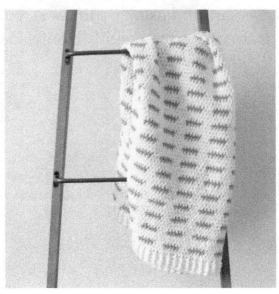

Crochet Modern Bunny Lovey

It did take me three attempts to get it all sorted out. At first, I thought I might have to settle and have it just be a pillow, which still is an option for you if you like, just don't make it as wide. But I really wanted this to be a blanket.

MATERIALS

Finished size of the lovey/blanket is 24×26 (If you choose to use this graph as a C2C, but use size 4 weight yarn, I'm estimating based on my other C2C's I've done that your blanket would turn out somewhere in the 36 to 40 inch square range. If you use the chunky weight yarn, it will be even bigger.)

2 skeins of **Bernat Softee Baby Chunky in Fluffy Cloud White**

2 skeins of **Bernat Softee Baby Chunky in Cozy Grey**

Size L and K hooks, I liked switching to K for the first round of the border to eliminate ruffling, I'll explain more below.

Scissors

Tapestry needle to weave in the ends.

PATTERN

Chain the first 18 chains in grey, pull through and chain the next 16 chains in white, pull through and chain the remaining 18 chains in grey, chain 1 more for the turning chain. (53 chains total)

Now start following the graph working from the bottom up. The base chain row is not shown on the graph.

Use a Single Crochet (SC) stitch to work the graph.

When you are finished with all 52 rows, weave in all the ends that you have so far before you start the border.

BORDER

Change to a K size hook, (one size smaller) and start on a corner that will have you work down one side. Pull up a loop with the white yarn, and work one SC (single crochet-US terms) per row. Work SC-CH-SC into each corner. When you return to the starting corner, work one SC, CH and join to the first SC you made with a slip stitch, CH 1 and turn, and change back to your L size hook. Work one more SC into the corner space and now continue around in the opposite direction. Always work SC-CH-SC into the corner CH space.

Hopefully, this method of switching to a smaller size hook for the first row of the border will help you make the border straighter. You are also free to put what ever border you wish. I think a shell border like the one worked in the **purple gingham blanket** would be nice,

or the ruffle border that is worked in the **C2C heart blanket** would look really well too.

I hope your modern bunny lovey turns out amazing any way you choose to finish it!

Crochet Petal Stitch Baby Blanket

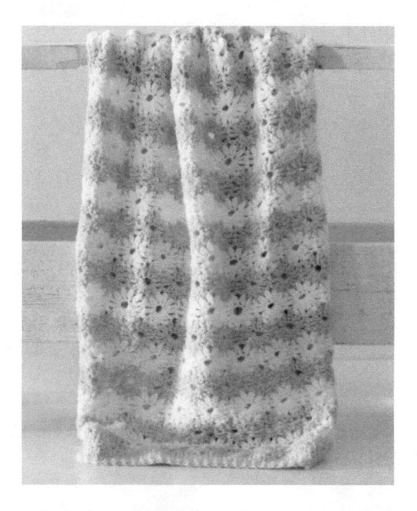

I was look through swatches of yarn colors and when I saw this peach blossom next to the baby grey, I knew immediately that the classic crochet petal stitch would look beautiful!

I love the extra pop of a row of white. Separating each color with grey worked well to set them apart and give the illusion of daisies!

MATERIALS

(Finished size 30 x 34 inches. All terms US)

Bernat Baby Sport Yarn in Peach Blossom, Baby Grey, and White. This is size 3 weight yarn, and these particular skeins they sent me were jumbo 1200 yards of yarn! One each was plenty. But if you are buying smaller, regular size, buy two of each color.

Size G hook. (Feel free to use the size you are comfortable using for size 3 baby sport yarn.)

Scissors

Tapestry needle to weave in the ends.

Fabric softener (the yarn needs to be softened up a bit after you are finished)

PATTERN

Chain 146 with baby grey, (pattern repeat is 11+3)

ROW 1: In the second Chain from the hook, single crochet (SC), Chain (CH) 1, Skip (SK) over the next CH, 1 SC into the next CH. *CH 3, SK over 3 CH, 1 SC into the next space (sp). CH 3, SK over 3 CH, 1 SC into the next sp. CH 2, SK 2 CH, 1 SC into the next CH. Repeat from * until 10 chains remain. Then CH 3, SK 3 CH, 1 SC in next sp, CH 3 again, SK 3 CH, 1 SC in the next sp, CH 1, SK 1, SC in the last space.

ROW 2: CH 3 and turn. In the first CH sp, work a double crochet 2 together cluster (CL), CH 2, CL. CH 1, SK over SC and CH 3's, 1 SC into next SC. *CH 1, SK over CH 3's and SK SC, CL into CH 2 sp. work "2 CH CL" 3 times in same CH 2 sp. CH 1. SK over CH 3's, 1 SC into next SC, repeat from * to last 7 spaces. CH 1, SK over CH 3's, into the last CH 1 sp, work "CL, 2 CH, CL" 1 dc into last SC pulling through with new color. (peach blossom)

ROW 3: CH 1 and turn. 1 SC into first dc, *CH 3, 1 CL into the tops of the next 4 CL's, CH 3, 1 SC into next 2 CH sp: repeat from * to the end, working last SC into top of turning CH.

ROW 4: CH 1 and turn. 1 SC into first SC, *CH 3, 1 SC into the top of next CL, CH 2, SK 2 CL, 1 SC into top of next CL, CH 3, 1 SC into next SC. repeat from * to the end.

ROW 5: CH 1 and turn, 1 SC into first SC. *CH 1, skip over 3 CHs, CL into next CH 2 sp. "CH 2, CL," 3 times in same CH 2 space. CH 1, SK over 3 CHs, 1 SC into next SC. repeat from *to the end, pulling through with new color. (baby grey)

ROW 6: CH 3 and turn. 1 CL into each of next two CL, CH 3, 1 SC in CH 2 sp, CH 3. *CL into next four CL, CH 3, 1 SC into CH 2 sp, CH 3, repeat from * to last 2 CL's, work 1 CL into each, 1 dc into last SC.

ROW 7: CH 1 and turn, 1 SC into first DC, CH 1, SK 1 CL, 1 SC into next CL, CH 3, 1 SC into next SC, CH 3, *1 SC into next CL, CH 2, SK 2 CL's, 1 SC into top of next CL. CH 3, 1 SC into next SC, CH 3 repeat from *to last 2 CL, 1 SC into next CL, CH 1, SK CL, 1 SC into top of turning chain.

Repeat rows 2 – 7, changing colors after row 2, alternating between peach blossom and white, and after row 5 back to baby grey.

6 rows of peach blossom, 5 rows of white and 10 complete rows of baby grey.

Stop after row 7 with a half way completed grey flower. Place a marker through this stitch, don't pull through and cut off, you'll be starting the border from this point.

Before starting the border, weave in all the ends with your tapestry needle, working in and out of the loops several times, then cutting the yarn close to the blanket to hide the end.

BORDER

Start at the last stitch you made, CH 3 and turn. dc into the same stitch. Work 3 DC in the next CH 3 space, SK over the SC, DC 3 into the next CH 3 space. SK over the next SC, work 2 DC into the CH 2 space. Continue across the entire row working in this manner. When you get to the next corner, work 1 DC into the CH 1 space and then 3 DC into the SC.

Now work the side of the blanket paying close attention to working one DC per SC and 2 DC around a DC post or CH 3. Try as best you can to keep these stitches even. When you get to the next corner, DC 3 into the corner stitch.

Work across the bottom of the blanket in the same manner you did at the top, 3 DC into CH 3 spaces, skip over SC's, and 2 DC into CH 2 spaces. Don't forget the CH 1 spaces at the beginning and end of the row. Work 3 DC into the corner.

Work back up the side in the same manner as listed above.

Work one final DC into the space where you started with CH 3 and 1 DC. Slip stitch into the top of the CH 3. CH 1 and turn.

SC into each DC around, working 3 SC into each corner. Join with a slip stitch to complete the round, CH 1 and turn. Work 5 rounds of SC.

OPTIONAL (Substitute the final 3 rounds in mesh stitch. I chained 1 and turned, worked 1 SC, CH 1, SK over 1 CH, 1 SC into the next. Repeating this pattern around, working SC, CH 1, SC into each corner. Slip stitch to join, CH 1 and turn. SC into the top of SC, CH 1, SK over CH 1, SC into the top of SC, repeating around, working "SC, CH 1, SC" into the middle CH 1 space of each corner.)

Finished!